Thinking Inside the Block:

THE TEACHER'S DAY-PLANNER

Pam Robbins
Lynne E. Herndon

CORWIN PRESS, INC.
A Sage Publications Company
Thousand Oaks, California

Copyright ©1998 by Corwin Press, Inc.

All rights reserved. Use of handouts, resources, and sample documents is authorized for individual teachers for their personal use only. Except for that usage, no part of this book may be reproduced or utilized in any form or by any means, electronic or mechanical, including photocopying, recording, or by any information storage and retrieval system, without permission in writing from the publisher.

For information:

Corwin Press, Inc.
A Sage Publications Company
2455 Teller Road
Thousand Oaks, California 91320
E-mail: order@corwinpress.com

SAGE Publications Ltd.
6 Bonhill Street
London EC2A 4PU
United Kingdom

SAGE Publications India Pvt. Ltd.
M-32 Market
Greater Kailash I
New Delhi 110 048 India

Library of Congress Cataloging-in-Publication Data

ISBN 0-8039-6780-2

This book is printed on acid-free paper.

98 99 00 01 02 10 9 8 7 6 5 4 3 2 1

Production Editor: S. Marlene Head
Editorial Assistant: Kristen L. Gibson
Cover Designer: Michelle Lee

CONTENTS

- About the Authors
- Introduction

Teacher Data Sheets
- Teacher Information Form
- Professional Development Record

Calendars
- Year-at-a-Glance
- Month-at-a-Glance

Address Book

Website Directory

Software Inventory

Video Inventory

Text/Materials Check-Out Sheets

Seating Charts

Student Special Needs Forms

Student Responsibility Forms

Student Assignment Sheets

Parent/Student Request for Make-Up Work Forms

Communication Records
- Teacher/Parent Communication Records
- Teacher and Student Communication Slips
- Ways to Add Variety to Saying "Good for You"

Helpful Hints for the Substitute Teacher

Student Information Forms

Class Attendance Forms

Class Assignments Forms

Class Grade Forms

Lesson Planning Forms
- Inventory of Teaching Strategies
- Reflection Pages

Tips: Taking Care of Yourself

ABOUT THE AUTHORS

This lesson planning guide was conceptualized by two educators: Pam Robbins, an educational consultant, and Lynne E. Herndon, a veteran classroom teacher. It represents a response to educators who have expressed a need for an organized, practical, and comprehensive way to plan for all aspects of classroom instruction, in a time-efficient manner.

Pam Robbins consults internationally in the areas of instructional strategies for block scheduling, brain-compatible teaching approaches, emotional intelligence, peer coaching, supervision, leadership, school improvement, and presentation skills. Her clients include local school districts, state departments of education, universities, leadership academies, the Department of Defense Education Activity, and corporations throughout the world. She also works with professional organizations such as the National Staff Development Council, the Association for Supervision and Curriculum Development, the American Association for Administrators in South America, and the American Society for Training and Development.

Robbins has written three books: *How to Plan and Implement a Peer Coaching Program* (ASCD, 1991); *The Principal's Companion*, with coauthor Harvey Alvy (Corwin Press, 1995); and *If I Only Knew* with coauthor Harvey Alvy (Corwin Press, 1998). She also developed a *Professional Inquiry Kit on Emotional Intelligence* (ASCD, 1997).

Robbins is a former classroom teacher. Her educational background includes a bachelor's degree in English from the University of California, a master's degree in education from California State University, Sacramento, and a doctorate from the University of California, Berkeley. Robbins may be contacted by phone: (540) 828-0107; fax: (540) 828-2326; e-mail: probbins@shentel.net.

Lynne E. Herndon has spent the past 15 years teaching science at Fort Dodge Senior High School, Fort Dodge, Iowa. Fort Dodge Senior High has been using the block schedule since 1995. Herndon was very active in the school reform process at Fort Dodge Senior High. Since she began teaching in the block, she has conducted several workshops in the area of classroom management, lesson planning for extended periods, and the development of instructional strategies for teaching in a block schedule.

Herndon's educational background includes a bachelor of science degree from Buena Vista College, Storm Lake, Iowa, and a master's degree in science education from the University of Northern Iowa.

Herndon may be contacted by phone: (515) 222-5842; fax: (515) 222-5841; e-mail: lynne.herndon@mci2000.com.

INTRODUCTION

This guide evolved as a consequence of two educators' desire to create a lesson planning book where everything teachers need is in one place, with the flexibility to arrange the pages as they see fit. In this way, the book can be responsive to a wide spectrum of teacher styles, beliefs, and values. The binder format allows individuals to add or delete pages as well. The printed tabbed pages correspond to the headings in the Table of Contents; you can insert them in order or rearrange them to suit your needs.

The guide was originally designed for teachers who teach in a block schedule. However, many educators remarked that its contents would be applicable to those teaching in a traditional schedule as well. Hence, the title evolved to be **Thinking Inside the Block: The Teacher's Day-Planner.**

The contents of the guide include:

- **Teacher Information** form for name, address, fax, phone, e-mail address, and schedule.
- **Professional Development** record with space to write in professional goals, classes, workshops, conferences, and inservices attended.
- **Calendar** section with a year-at-a-glance calendar as well as month-at-a-glance calendars.
- **Address Book** for names, addresses, and phone and fax numbers, as well as e-mail addresses.
- **Website Directory** with examples of Websites as well as a place to add one's own.
- **Software Inventory** pages to record one's software library.
- **Video Inventory** pages to make note of one's video collection.
- **Text/Materials Check-Out Sheet** to record which text has been checked out, to whom, and in what condition.
- **Seating Chart** for recording one's room arrangement, with samples of different seating configurations.

- **Student Special Needs** form for recording information about students with medical or behavioral needs.

- **Student Responsibility** form, a black line master that can be used to promote student responsibility with regard to attendance, coming to class prepared with appropriate materials, class participation, and assignment completion.

- **Student Assignment Sheets,** a black line master designed for students to record daily assignments and due dates. Also provided is a space to enter the date assignments are completed, whether they were late or on time, and the grade/points received.

- **Parent/Student Request for Make-Up Work**, a black line master that provides a way to communicate about assignments and corresponding directions necessary to complete missed work.

- **Communication Records** provide space to record the dates and content of phone conversations and meetings that may be referenced at a future time.

- **Communication Slips** to facilitate two-way dialogue between teacher and student in a time-efficient manner. These slips are also presented as black line masters with suggestions for use.

- **Helpful Hints for the Substitute Teacher** is a form on which one can note the location of specific items, individuals to call upon to answer questions, and a daily schedule.

- **Student Information** forms with space to write in student names, identification numbers, grade level, counselor's name, address, and phone number.

- **Attendance** pages are provided as black line masters to record student attendance information.

- **Class Assignments** forms with space to write in the assignments given and a brief description of each.

- **Class Grade** forms are provided as black line masters on which to record data about assignments and corresponding grades in a practical, time-efficient way.

- **Lesson Planning** forms offer a comprehensive, practical way to organize teaching plans. At the back of this section is a place to record one's repertoire of teaching strategies, and notes suggesting how they might be used.

- **Inventory of Teaching Strategies** provides a quick reference to add variety and novelty to lessons.
- **Reflection** pages offer a place to record thoughts, perceptions, or impressions about how a lesson worked, what modifications might be indicated if this lesson is used in the future, and any other notes about the teaching experience.
- **Tips: Taking Care of Yourself** is a brief section of ideas that teacher colleagues have shared about taking care of number one -- you! Teaching is a labor intensive, highly sophisticated, demanding activity. It takes a lot out of an individual. So, it follows that there's a need to take care of oneself so there's fuel for the daily rigor of the profession.

This guide can be used in several ways. Teachers can organize the pages to fit their needs. Many teachers are experiencing teaching in extended periods of time. Due to the large variety of schedules in use by schools implementing "the block," the number of classes a teacher might teach varies tremendously. For this reason, teachers may make as many copies of the enclosed sheets as they need for their class records. The format allows one to arrange the pages in a variety of ways and also provides those teachers using electronic grading a place to insert their copies of the grade book. Answer keys and blank masters of class materials may also be inserted.

It is hoped that collectively these pages will offer a comprehensive, flexible way of responding to the daily, monthly, and yearly challenges and opportunities of teaching, in a practical, time efficient manner. Enjoy!

> "I touch
> the future...
> I teach"

— Christa McAuliffe

TEACHER INFORMATION FORM

Name _____

School _____

School Address _____

Phone Number _____

Fax Number _____

E-Mail Address _____

Schedule	**Current School Year:**

Thinking Inside the Block: The Teacher's Day-Planner
by P. Robbins and L. Herndon. Copyright © Corwin Press, 1998.

PROFESSIONAL DEVELOPMENT RECORD

Professional goals for the year:

Professional organizations/memberships/subscriptions:

Classes/Conferences/Workshops/Inservices Attended	New Ideas

YEAR-AT-A-GLANCE

Use this form to note key dates: for example, end of semester, parent conferences, holidays, testing schedules, inservice days.

August

September

October

November

December

January

February

March

April

May

June

July

Thinking Inside the Block: The Teacher's Day-Planner
by P. Robbins and L. Herndon. Copyright © Corwin Press, 1998.

August

Monday	Tuesday	Wednesday	Thursday	Friday	Sat/Sun

Thinking Inside the Block: The Teacher's Day-Planner by P. Robbins and L. Herndon. Copyright © Corwin Press, 1998.

September

Monday	Tuesday	Wednesday	Thursday	Friday	Sat/Sun

Thinking Inside the Block: The Teacher's Day-Planner by P. Robbins and L. Herndon. Copyright © Corwin Press, 1998.

October

Monday	Tuesday	Wednesday	Thursday	Friday	Sat/Sun

Thinking Inside the Block: The Teacher's Day-Planner by P. Robbins and L. Herndon. Copyright © Corwin Press, 1998.

November

Monday	Tuesday	Wednesday	Thursday	Friday	Sat/Sun

Thinking Inside the Block: The Teacher's Day-Planner by P. Robbins and L. Herndon. Copyright © Corwin Press, 1998.

December

Monday	Tuesday	Wednesday	Thursday	Friday	Sat/Sun

Thinking Inside the Block: The Teacher's Day-Planner
by P. Robbins and L. Herndon. Copyright © Corwin Press, 1998.

January

Monday	Tuesday	Wednesday	Thursday	Friday	Sat/Sun

Thinking Inside the Block: The Teacher's Day-Planner by P. Robbins and L. Herndon. Copyright © Corwin Press, 1998.

February

Monday	Tuesday	Wednesday	Thursday	Friday	Sat/Sun

Thinking Inside the Block: The Teacher's Day-Planner by P. Robbins and L. Herndon. Copyright © Corwin Press, 1998.

March

Monday	Tuesday	Wednesday	Thursday	Friday	Sat/Sun

Thinking Inside the Block: The Teacher's Day-Planner by P. Robbins and L. Herndon. Copyright © Corwin Press, 1998.

April

Monday	Tuesday	Wednesday	Thursday	Friday	Sat/Sun

Thinking Inside the Block: The Teacher's Day-Planner by P. Robbins and L. Herndon. Copyright © Corwin Press, 1998.

May

Monday	Tuesday	Wednesday	Thursday	Friday	Sat/Sun

Thinking Inside the Block: The Teacher's Day-Planner by P. Robbins and L. Herndon. Copyright © Corwin Press, 1998.

June

Monday	Tuesday	Wednesday	Thursday	Friday	Sat/Sun

Thinking Inside the Block: The Teacher's Day-Planner by P. Robbins and L. Herndon. Copyright © Corwin Press, 1998.

July

Monday	Tuesday	Wednesday	Thursday	Friday	Sat/Sun

Thinking Inside the Block: The Teacher's Day-Planner
by P. Robbins and L. Herndon. Copyright © Corwin Press, 1998.

ADDRESS BOOK

Name	Address	Phone No.	Fax No.	E-Mail

Thinking Inside the Block: The Teacher's Day-Planner by P. Robbins and L. Herndon. Copyright © Corwin Press, 1998.

ADDRESS BOOK

Name	Address	Phone No.	Fax No.	E-Mail

Thinking Inside the Block: The Teacher's Day-Planner by P. Robbins and L. Herndon. Copyright © Corwin Press, 1998.

WEBSITE DIRECTORY

Block Scheduling:

http://carei.coled.umn.edu/bsmain.htm
http://www.classroom.net/classweb/myhome.html
http://www.aasa.org/block.htm

Study Skills:

http://www.nj.com/education/instructor/study1.html
http://www.adm.uwaterloo.ca/infocs/study/learn.html

News / Weather

http://www.cnn.com
http://www.weather.com
http://www.usatoday.com

Favorites:

Education:

http://ericir.syr.edu
http://www.gsh.org
http://thechalkboard.com
http://www.aaas.org/enr.sen/nvgt.htm
http://www.classroom.net

Reference:

http://www.superlibrary.com

Shareware:

http://www.shareware.com
http://www.jumbo.com

Thinking Inside the Block: The Teacher's Day-Planner
by P. Robbins and L. Herndon. Copyright © Corwin Press, 1998.

WEBSITE DIRECTORY

Thinking Inside the Block: The Teacher's Day-Planner by P. Robbins and L. Herndon. Copyright © Corwin Press, 1998.

SOFTWARE INVENTORY

Title	Description	Media Type	Application	License

Thinking Inside the Block: The Teacher's Day-Planner by P. Robbins and L. Herndon. Copyright © Corwin Press, 1998.

VIDEO INVENTORY

Title	Description	Length	Applicable Unit	Date Produced/Date Recorded

Thinking Inside the Block: The Teacher's Day-Planner by P. Robbins and L. Herndon. Copyright © Corwin Press, 1998.

TEXT/MATERIALS CHECK-OUT SHEET

Class_____ **Period**_____

Item Description, i.e., text/author

Checked Out to:	Item Number:	Condition				
		NEW	EXCEL	GOOD	FAIR	POOR

Thinking Inside the Block: The Teacher's Day-Planner
by P. Robbins and L. Herndon. Copyright © Corwin Press, 1998.

TEXT/MATERIALS CHECK-OUT SHEET

Class_____ **Period**_____

Item Description, i.e., text/author

Condition

Checked Out to:	Item Number:	NEW	EXCEL	GOOD	FAIR	POOR

Thinking Inside the Block: The Teacher's Day-Planner
by P. Robbins and L. Herndon. Copyright © Corwin Press, 1998.

TEXT/MATERIALS CHECK-OUT SHEET

Class_____ Period_____

Item Description, i.e., text/author

Condition
NEW	EXCEL	GOOD	FAIR	POOR

Checked Out to:	Item Number:	NEW	EXCEL	GOOD	FAIR	POOR

Thinking Inside the Block: The Teacher's Day-Planner
by P. Robbins and L. Herndon. Copyright © Corwin Press, 1998.

TEXT/MATERIALS CHECK-OUT SHEET

Class_____ Period_____

Condition

Item Description, i.e., text/author

Checked Out to:	Item Number:	NEW	EXCEL	GOOD	FAIR	POOR

Thinking Inside the Block: The Teacher's Day-Planner
by P. Robbins and L. Herndon. Copyright © Corwin Press, 1998.

TEXT/MATERIALS CHECK-OUT SHEET

Class_____ Period_____

Item Description, i.e., text/author

Checked Out to:	Item Number:	Condition				
		NEW	EXCEL	GOOD	FAIR	POOR

Thinking Inside the Block: The Teacher's Day-Planner
by P. Robbins and L. Herndon. Copyright © Corwin Press, 1998.

TEXT/MATERIALS CHECK-OUT SHEET

Class_____ **Period**_____

Item Description, i.e., text/author

Checked Out to:	Item Number:	Condition				
		NEW	EXCEL	GOOD	FAIR	POOR

Thinking Inside the Block: The Teacher's Day-Planner
by P. Robbins and L. Herndon. Copyright © Corwin Press, 1998.

SEATING CHARTS

Suggestions for Use

There are many ways to organize the classroom. A teacher's style, values and beliefs, classroom activities, available furniture, and size of the room all influence the decision about room arrangement. Indeed, how furniture is arranged can make or break the success of an activity. For this reason, there are a number of styles from which to choose.

When arranging classroom furniture, there are three general factors to consider: visibility, accessibility, and monitoring. Visibility addresses the question, "Can students see the instructor or areas of the room where instructional materials are located?" Accessibility pertains to whether materials are easily accessed. Monitoring ease is a critical consideration so that the teacher can oversee student work in progress or instructional centers. *

The following form offers a standard format upon which several seating configurations can be drawn: traditional, seating in pairs, group arrangements, dialogue circle, double aisle, and open forum.

There are several software applications on the market for record-keeping that incorporate seating charts. These allow one to develop templates for seating of students. Also included is the option to import student photographs into the charts. Substitute teachers welcome this option as they can put faces to names very quickly.

*Source: Carolyn Evertson, Professor, Peabody College, Nashville, Tennessee.

SEATING CHART

Class_____ **Period**_____ **Room**_____

Notes:
_____
_____
_____
_____
_____
_____

Thinking Inside the Block: The Teacher's Day-Planner
by P. Robbins and L. Herndon. Copyright © Corwin Press, 1998.

SEATING CHART

Class_____ **Period**_____ **Room**_____

Notes:
_____
_____
_____
_____
_____
_____
_____

Thinking Inside the Block: The Teacher's Day-Planner
by P. Robbins and L. Herndon. Copyright © Corwin Press, 1998.

SEATING CHART

Class_____ Period_____ Room_____

Notes:
_____
_____
_____
_____
_____
_____

Thinking Inside the Block: The Teacher's Day-Planner
by P. Robbins and L. Herndon. Copyright © Corwin Press, 1998.

SEATING CHART

Class_____ **Period**_____ **Room**_____

Notes:
_____
_____
_____
_____
_____
_____

Thinking Inside the Block: The Teacher's Day-Planner
by P. Robbins and L. Herndon. Copyright © Corwin Press, 1998.

SEATING CHART

Class_____ **Period**_____ **Room**_____

Notes:
_____
_____
_____
_____
_____
_____
_____

Thinking Inside the Block: The Teacher's Day-Planner
by P. Robbins and L. Herndon. Copyright © Corwin Press, 1998.

SEATING CHART

Class_____ **Period**_____ **Room**_____

Notes:
_____
_____
_____
_____
_____
_____

Thinking Inside the Block: The Teacher's Day-Planner
by P. Robbins and L. Herndon. Copyright © Corwin Press, 1998.

CUSTOM SEATING CHART

Thinking Inside the Block: The Teacher's Day-Planner
by P. Robbins and L. Herndon. Copyright © Corwin Press, 1998.

CUSTOM SEATING CHART

Thinking Inside the Block: The Teacher's Day-Planner
by P. Robbins and L. Herndon. Copyright © Corwin Press, 1998.

CUSTOM SEATING CHART

Thinking Inside the Block: The Teacher's Day-Planner
by P. Robbins and L. Herndon. Copyright © Corwin Press, 1998.

CUSTOM SEATING CHART

Thinking Inside the Block: The Teacher's Day-Planner
by P. Robbins and L. Herndon. Copyright © Corwin Press, 1998.

CUSTOM SEATING CHART

Thinking Inside the Block: The Teacher's Day-Planner
by P. Robbins and L. Herndon. Copyright © Corwin Press, 1998.

CUSTOM SEATING CHART

Thinking Inside the Block: The Teacher's Day-Planner
by P. Robbins and L. Herndon. Copyright © Corwin Press, 1998.

STUDENT SPECIAL NEEDS FORMS

Suggestions for Use

Use these forms to record reminders about specific students. For example, because of vision or hearing problems, do certain students need to be seated in the front of the room? Are there students who have been labeled as manifesting attention deficit disorder who would benefit from sitting in a specific location? Are there students who have special health needs or are on medication?

STUDENT SPECIAL NEEDS FORM

Student	Notes: Special Needs

STUDENT SPECIAL NEEDS FORM

Student	Notes: Special Needs

Thinking Inside the Block: The Teacher's Day-Planner
by P. Robbins and L. Herndon. Copyright © Corwin Press, 1998.

STUDENT SPECIAL NEEDS FORM

Student	Notes: Special Needs

STUDENT SPECIAL NEEDS FORM

Student	Notes: Special Needs

STUDENT SPECIAL NEEDS FORM

Student	Notes: Special Needs

STUDENT SPECIAL NEEDS FORM

Student	Notes: Special Needs

STUDENT RESPONSIBILITY FORMS

Suggestions for Use

Teachers may want to reproduce these forms on card stock. Some teachers color code for individual classes. Every student is given a form at the beginning of the semester. At this time, the concept of the card can be explained to the student. This provides an opportunity for the teacher to discuss the importance of good attendance, bringing materials to class, time on task, and turning in assignments to the teacher. Some teachers involve the students in the entire process by collaboratively establishing a simple rubric that can be used to record information on the cards. Having the students brainstorm the indicators to establish the criteria from which rubrics can be developed establishes student ownership. The teacher and class can then decide about the marking system they will use.

As students enter the classroom each day, they pull their cards from an in-tray or box where they are stored. The students complete the sections titled Attendance and Materials as the teacher takes roll. Following roll, the teacher can clip all make-up work to the cards of absent students and place them back in the in-tray. At the end of the period, the students complete the Participation and Assignments sections and return the cards to the in-tray as they leave the classroom.

There are several ways of using this form. However, it will only be effective if the criteria are clearly defined for the student. For example, students need to know what "being on task" means and what the teacher's expectations are.

This can also be a very useful tool for the teacher to determine how much time needs to be allotted for assignments. For example, if the majority of students mark their cards with a 2 in the assignment box, more time is needed for them to complete the assignment.

Student Name: _____ **Class:** _____

Attendance/Tardiness

Week	Mon.	Tues.	Wed.	Thu.	Fri.
1					
2					
3					
4					
5					
6					
7					
8					
9					
10					

Materials

Week	Mon.	Tues.	Wed.	Thu.	Fri.
1					
2					
3					
4					
5					
6					
7					
8					
9					
10					

Task/Participation

Week	Mon.	Tues.	Wed.	Thu.	Fri.
1					
2					
3					
4					
5					
6					
7					
8					
9					
10					

Assignments

Week	Mon.	Tues.	Wed.	Thu.	Fri.
1					
2					
3					
4					
5					
6					
7					
8					
9					
10					

Comments

Times for Detentions/Extra Help

Thinking Inside the Block: The Teacher's Day-Planner
by P. Robbins and L. Herndon. Copyright © Corwin Press, 1998.

Student Name: _____   Class: _____

Attendance/Tardiness

Week	Mon.	Tues.	Wed.	Thu.	Fri.
1					
2					
3					
4					
5					
6					
7					
8					
9					
10					

Materials

Week	Mon.	Tues.	Wed.	Thu.	Fri.
1					
2					
3					
4					
5					
6					
7					
8					
9					
10					

Task/Participation

Week	Mon.	Tues.	Wed.	Thu.	Fri.
1					
2					
3					
4					
5					
6					
7					
8					
9					
10					

Assignments

Week	Mon.	Tues.	Wed.	Thu.	Fri.
1					
2					
3					
4					
5					
6					
7					
8					
9					
10					

Comments

Times for Detentions/Extra Help

Thinking Inside the Block: The Teacher's Day-Planner
by P. Robbins and L. Herndon. Copyright © Corwin Press, 1998.

STUDENT RESPONSIBILITY CARD: SAMPLE RUBRICS

Suggestions for Use

- **Attendance:** Students can mark these according to the teacher's instruction. For example, P – present, A – absent, T – tardy, and so forth.

- **Materials:**

    1. Student has not brought any materials to class.
    2. Student has writing materials only.
    3. Student has writing materials and notebook.
    4. Student has writing materials, notebook, and textbook.

- **Participation:**

    1. Student is on task 0-25% of the time.
    2. Student is on task 26-50% of the time.
    3. Student is on task 51-75% of the time.
    4. Student is on task 76-100% of the time.

- **Assignments:**

    1. Assignment 0-25% completed.
    2. Assignment 26-50% completed.
    3. Assignment 51-75% completed.
    4. Assignment 76-100% completed.

Thinking Inside the Block: The Teacher's Day-Planner
by P. Robbins and L. Herndon. Copyright © Corwin Press, 1998.

STUDENT ASSIGNMENT SHEETS

Suggestions for Use

These sheets can be copied onto the back of students' responsibility cards, as previously discussed. Students can keep track of assignments as to when they were given, when they are due, if they were submitted on time or late, and the points or grades earned. These sheets can be useful to share with parents at conferences should any questions arise concerning assignment time frames.

These sheets also allow the teacher to identify students early in the semester who have a tendency to turn in late work or lose assignments and are generally disorganized. The information provided in these sheets can help students improve their organization skills and become more responsible toward their work.

STUDENT ASSIGNMENT SHEET

Name: Class:

Name of Assignment	Date Assgn	Due Date	On Time	Late	Late Date	Pts. Earn. Pts. Poss.	A	B	C	D	F

Thinking Inside the Block: The Teacher's Day-Planner
by P. Robbins and L. Herndon. Copyright © Corwin Press, 1998.

STUDENT ASSIGNMENT SHEET

Name: Class:

Name of Assignment	Date Assgn	Due Date	On Time	Late	Late Date	Pts. Earn. Pts. Poss.	A	B	C	D	F

Thinking Inside the Block: The Teacher's Day-Planner
by P. Robbins and L. Herndon. Copyright © Corwin Press, 1998.

PARENT/STUDENT REQUEST FORMS FOR MAKE-UP WORK

Suggestions for Use

The form that follows can be used to record briefly what was done in class and related work assigned during a student's absence. It can be used as a cover sheet and clipped to the student responsibility card to provide written instructions for the assignments or any other information that the teacher may wish to convey to the student.

We Miss You !

We are sorry that you have not been able to join us for class. Here are some of the assignments you have missed. Hope to see you soon.

Assignments/Instructions:

Other:

COMMUNICATION RECORDS

Suggestions for Use

Many teachers have found it useful to have a place where notes about phone conversations, conferences, or parent requests can be recorded. Such documentation is often useful for student progress reports or parent conferences. Sometimes this information can be valuable in communications with the principal, counselor, or student adviser.

TEACHER/PARENT COMMUNICATION RECORD

Student Name	Parent Name	Date	Notes/Parental Requests/Teacher Recommendations

Thinking Inside the Block: The Teacher's Day-Planner
by P. Robbins and L. Herndon. Copyright © Corwin Press, 1998.

TEACHER/PARENT COMMUNICATION RECORD

Student Name	Parent Name	Date	Notes/Parental Requests/Teacher Recommendations

TEACHER/PARENT COMMUNICATION RECORD

Student Name	Parent Name	Date	Notes/Parental Requests/Teacher Recommendations

TEACHER/PARENT COMMUNICATION RECORD

Student Name	Parent Name	Date	Notes/Parental Requests/Teacher Recommendations

Thinking Inside the Block: The Teacher's Day-Planner
by P. Robbins and L. Herndon. Copyright © Corwin Press, 1998.

TEACHER/PARENT COMMUNICATION RECORD

Student Name	Parent Name	Date	Notes/Parental Requests/Teacher Recommendations

TEACHER/PARENT COMMUNICATION RECORD

Student Name	Parent Name	Date	Notes/Parental Requests/Teacher Recommendations

Thinking Inside the Block: The Teacher's Day-Planner
by P. Robbins and L. Herndon. Copyright © Corwin Press, 1998.

COMMUNICATION SLIPS

Suggestions for Use

These slips can provide an additional time-efficient way to communicate with students and build relationships with them simultaneously. Students may use a similar approach to communicate with the teacher. There may be slips with headings such as "I'm confused about . . ." "I did not understand about . . ." " It would help if . . ." and "I would like to come in for extra help . . ." These slips can be attached to the Student Responsibility card, or the teacher might have a box in which students place their slips. Color coding these in bright colors will enable the teacher to see at a glance which students have indicated a need for attention or feedback.

| Could we . . . | I am confused about . . . |

I would like to come in for extra help with . . .

To increase my comfort level . . .

| I will be absent on _____ because . . . | It would help if . . . |

Thinking Inside the Block: The Teacher's Day-Planner
by P. Robbins and L. Herndon. Copyright © Corwin Press, 1998.

Daily Reminder:	**Awesome!**

Please see me . . .

How you've improved! Great job! Keep it up!

News Flash ! ! !	**You got my attention because . . .**

Thinking Inside the Block: The Teacher's Day-Planner
by P. Robbins and L. Herndon. Copyright © Corwin Press, 1998.

WAYS TO ADD VARIETY TO SAYING "GOOD FOR YOU!"

Suggestions for Use

Students are motivated by specific feedback that provides them with knowledge of results about their efforts. Often, however, teachers remark that they wish to find alternatives to the same old comment, "Good for you!" The purpose of 50 Ways to Say "Good for You!" is to provide a variety of ways to acknowledge work well done. Specific feedback, supplied by the teacher, should follow each of these comments (e.g., "Wow! The story you composed captured my interest immediately with your use of adjectives in the opening paragraph!").

50 Ways to Say "Good for You!"

- Awesome!
- Great job!
- You got my attention!
- Thumbs up!
- Wow!
- Fantastic!
- Fabulous!
- Captivating!
- Wonderful!
- It's been a pleasure!
- What great work!
- Amazing!
- Super!
- You're really "on"!
- Excellent!
- Outrageous!
- Impressive!
- Inspiring!
- This has merit!
- Grand!
- Distinguished work!
- Impeccable!
- Delightful!
- What a brainstorm!
- Brilliant!
- Punctual and perfect!
- Superb!
- You're a star!
- You got my attention!
- Perfect!
- Gorgeous job!
- What a treat to read this paper!
- You really worked hard! It shows!
- You made it!
- Keep on truckin! This is great!
- Celebrate! This is excellent work!
- I salute you! Superb job!
- You excelled on this one!
- You outdid yourself!
- You can be proud of this!
- Outstanding!
- Admirable work!
- First class!
- Superior!
- Well done!
- Quality work!
- Astonishing!
- Beautiful!
- Thoughtful!
- You've jumped the hurdles and finished in the limelight!

Thinking Inside the Block: The Teacher's Day-Planner
by P. Robbins and L. Herndon. Copyright © Corwin Press, 1998.

HELPFUL HINTS FOR THE SUBSTITUTE TEACHER

Suggestions for Use

The form that follows is designed to enable the substitute teacher to locate materials critical to conducting each class. It also communicates information about the regular teacher's schedule, special classroom procedures, dependable students, and teachers who can assist the substitute teacher. Together, the two parts of this form will contribute to a meaningful experience for both substitute teacher and students.

HELPFUL HINTS FOR THE SUBSTITUTE TEACHER

Classroom Teacher Name_____ Room_____

You will find the following essential items in the place indicated:

Item	Location
Grade Book	
Seating Chart	
Attendance Sheets	
Teaching Materials	
Lesson Plans	
Emergency Lesson Plans	
Hall Passes	
Referrals	

My schedule is as follows:

Dependable students in my class:

A teacher who can help:

Special procedures:

Thinking Inside the Block: The Teacher's Day-Planner
by P. Robbins and L. Herndon. Copyright © Corwin Press, 1998.

STUDENT INFORMATION FORM

Teacher Name	Class and Section	School Year	Semester

Student	ID #	Grade	Counselor	Address	Phone #

Thinking Inside the Block: The Teacher's Day-Planner
by P. Robbins and L. Herndon. Copyright © Corwin Press, 1998.

STUDENT INFORMATION FORM

Teacher Name	Class and Section	School Year	Semester

Student	ID #	Grade	Counselor	Address	Phone #

Thinking Inside the Block: The Teacher's Day-Planner
by P. Robbins and L. Herndon. Copyright © Corwin Press, 1998.

STUDENT INFORMATION FORM

Teacher Name	Class and Section	School Year	Semester

Student	ID #	Grade	Counselor	Address	Phone #

Thinking Inside the Block: The Teacher's Day-Planner
by P. Robbins and L. Herndon. Copyright © Corwin Press, 1998.

STUDENT INFORMATION FORM

Teacher Name	Class and Section	School Year	Semester

Student	ID #	Grade	Counselor	Address	Phone #

Thinking Inside the Block: The Teacher's Day-Planner
by P. Robbins and L. Herndon. Copyright © Corwin Press, 1998.

STUDENT INFORMATION FORM

Teacher Name	Class and Section	School Year	Semester

Student	ID #	Grade	Counselor	Address	Phone #

Thinking Inside the Block: The Teacher's Day-Planner
by P. Robbins and L. Herndon. Copyright © Corwin Press, 1998.

STUDENT INFORMATION FORM

| Teacher Name | Class and Section | School Year | Semester |

Student	ID #	Grade	Counselor	Address	Phone #

Thinking Inside the Block: The Teacher's Day-Planner
by P. Robbins and L. Herndon. Copyright © Corwin Press, 1998.

CLASS ATTENDANCE

| Teacher Name | Class and Section | School Year | Semester |

Month/Date															
Day of Week	M	Tu	W	Th	F	M	Tu	W	Th	F	M	Tu	W	Th	F
Student Name															

Thinking Inside the Block: The Teacher's Day-Planner
by P. Robbins and L. Herndon. Copyright © Corwin Press, 1998.

CLASS ATTENDANCE

Teacher Name	Class and Section	School Year	Semester

Month/Date														
Day of Week	M	Tu	W	Th	F	M	Tu	W	Th	F	M	Tu	W	Th	F
Student Name															

Thinking Inside the Block: The Teacher's Day-Planner
by P. Robbins and L. Herndon. Copyright © Corwin Press, 1998.

CLASS ATTENDANCE

Teacher Name	Class and Section	School Year	Semester

Month/Date															
Day of Week	M	Tu	W	Th	F	M	Tu	W	Th	F	M	Tu	W	Th	F
Student Name															

Thinking Inside the Block: The Teacher's Day-Planner
by P. Robbins and L. Herndon. Copyright © Corwin Press, 1998.

CLASS ATTENDANCE

Teacher Name	Class and Section	School Year	Semester

Month/Date														
Day of Week	M	Tu	W	Th	F	M	Tu	W	Th	F	M	Tu	W	Th	F
Student Name															

Thinking Inside the Block: The Teacher's Day-Planner
by P. Robbins and L. Herndon. Copyright © Corwin Press, 1998.

CLASS ATTENDANCE

| Teacher Name | Class and Section | School Year | Semester |

Month/Date														
Day of Week	M	Tu	W	Th	F	M	Tu	W	Th	F	M	Tu	W	Th	F
Student Name															

Thinking Inside the Block: The Teacher's Day-Planner
by P. Robbins and L. Herndon. Copyright © Corwin Press, 1998.

CLASS ATTENDANCE

Teacher Name	Class and Section	School Year	Semester

Month/Date															
Day of Week	M	Tu	W	Th	F	M	Tu	W	Th	F	M	Tu	W	Th	F
Student Name															

Thinking Inside the Block: The Teacher's Day-Planner
by P. Robbins and L. Herndon. Copyright © Corwin Press, 1998.

CLASS ATTENDANCE

Teacher Name	Class and Section	School Year	Semester

Month/Date														
Day of Week	M	Tu	W	Th	F	M	Tu	W	Th	F	M	Tu	W	Th	F
Student Name															

Thinking Inside the Block: The Teacher's Day-Planner
by P. Robbins and L. Herndon. Copyright © Corwin Press, 1998.

CLASS ATTENDANCE

| Teacher Name | Class and Section | School Year | Semester |

Month/Date															
Day of Week	M	Tu	W	Th	F	M	Tu	W	Th	F	M	Tu	W	Th	F
Student Name															

Thinking Inside the Block: The Teacher's Day-Planner
by P. Robbins and L. Herndon. Copyright © Corwin Press, 1998.

CLASS ATTENDANCE

Teacher Name	Class and Section	School Year	Semester

Month/Date															
Day of Week	M	Tu	W	Th	F	M	Tu	W	Th	F	M	Tu	W	Th	F
Student Name															

Thinking Inside the Block: The Teacher's Day-Planner
by P. Robbins and L. Herndon. Copyright © Corwin Press, 1998.

CLASS ATTENDANCE

Teacher Name	Class and Section	School Year	Semester

Month/Date														
Day of Week	M	Tu	W	Th	F	M	Tu	W	Th	F	M	Tu	W	Th	F
Student Name															

Thinking Inside the Block: The Teacher's Day-Planner
by P. Robbins and L. Herndon. Copyright © Corwin Press, 1998.

CLASS ATTENDANCE

| Teacher Name | Class and Section | School Year | Semester |

Month/Date															
Day of Week	M	Tu	W	Th	F	M	Tu	W	Th	F	M	Tu	W	Th	F
Student Name															

Thinking Inside the Block: The Teacher's Day-Planner
by P. Robbins and L. Herndon. Copyright © Corwin Press, 1998.

CLASS ATTENDANCE

Teacher Name	Class and Section	School Year	Semester

Month/Date														
Day of Week	M	Tu	W	Th	F	M	Tu	W	Th	F	M	Tu	W	Th	F
Student Name															

Thinking Inside the Block: The Teacher's Day-Planner
by P. Robbins and L. Herndon. Copyright © Corwin Press, 1998.

CLASS ATTENDANCE

| Teacher Name | Class and Section | School Year | Semester |

Month/Date															
Day of Week	M	Tu	W	Th	F	M	Tu	W	Th	F	M	Tu	W	Th	F
Student Name															

Thinking Inside the Block: The Teacher's Day-Planner
by P. Robbins and L. Herndon. Copyright © Corwin Press, 1998.

CLASS ATTENDANCE

| Teacher Name | Class and Section | School Year | Semester |

Month/Date														
Day of Week	M	Tu	W	Th	F	M	Tu	W	Th	F	M	Tu	W	Th	F
Student Name															

Thinking Inside the Block: The Teacher's Day-Planner
by P. Robbins and L. Herndon. Copyright © Corwin Press, 1998.

CLASS ATTENDANCE

Teacher Name	Class and Section	School Year	Semester

Month/Date														
Day of Week	M	Tu	W	Th	F	M	Tu	W	Th	F	M	Tu	W	Th	F
Student Name														

Thinking Inside the Block: The Teacher's Day-Planner
by P. Robbins and L. Herndon. Copyright © Corwin Press, 1998.

CLASS ATTENDANCE

Teacher Name	Class and Section	School Year	Semester

Month/Date															
Day of Week	M	Tu	W	Th	F	M	Tu	W	Th	F	M	Tu	W	Th	F
Student Name															

Thinking Inside the Block: The Teacher's Day-Planner
by P. Robbins and L. Herndon. Copyright © Corwin Press, 1998.

CLASS ATTENDANCE

| Teacher Name | Class and Section | School Year | Semester |

Month/Date														
Day of Week	M	Tu	W	Th	F	M	Tu	W	Th	F	M	Tu	W	Th	F
Student Name															

Thinking Inside the Block: The Teacher's Day-Planner
by P. Robbins and L. Herndon. Copyright © Corwin Press, 1998.

CLASS ATTENDANCE

| Teacher Name | Class and Section | School Year | Semester |

Month/Date															
Day of Week	M	Tu	W	Th	F	M	Tu	W	Th	F	M	Tu	W	Th	F
Student Name															

Thinking Inside the Block: The Teacher's Day-Planner
by P. Robbins and L. Herndon. Copyright © Corwin Press, 1998.

CLASS ASSIGNMENTS

Teacher Name	**Class and Section**	**School Year**	**Semester**

#	Assignment	Description
1		
2		
3		
4		
5		
6		
7		
8		
9		
10		
11		
12		
13		
14		
15		
16		
17		
18		
19		
20		
21		
22		

Thinking Inside the Block: The Teacher's Day-Planner
by P. Robbins and L. Herndon. Copyright © Corwin Press, 1998.

CLASS ASSIGNMENTS

Teacher Name	Class and Section	School Year	Semester

#	Assignment	Description

Thinking Inside the Block: The Teacher's Day-Planner
by P. Robbins and L. Herndon. Copyright © Corwin Press, 1998.

CLASS ASSIGNMENTS

Teacher Name	Class and Section	School Year	Semester

#	Assignment	Description
1		
2		
3		
4		
5		
6		
7		
8		
9		
10		
11		
12		
13		
14		
15		
16		
17		
18		
19		
20		
21		
22		

Thinking Inside the Block: The Teacher's Day-Planner
by P. Robbins and L. Herndon. Copyright © Corwin Press, 1998.

CLASS ASSIGNMENTS

| Teacher Name | Class and Section | School Year | Semester |

#	Assignment	Description

Thinking Inside the Block: The Teacher's Day-Planner
by P. Robbins and L. Herndon. Copyright © Corwin Press, 1998.

CLASS ASSIGNMENTS

Teacher Name	Class and Section	School Year	Semester

#	Assignment	Description
1		
2		
3		
4		
5		
6		
7		
8		
9		
10		
11		
12		
13		
14		
15		
16		
17		
18		
19		
20		
21		
22		

Thinking Inside the Block: The Teacher's Day-Planner
by P. Robbins and L. Herndon. Copyright © Corwin Press, 1998.

CLASS ASSIGNMENTS

| Teacher Name | Class and Section | School Year | Semester |

#	Assignment	Description

Thinking Inside the Block: The Teacher's Day-Planner
by P. Robbins and L. Herndon. Copyright © Corwin Press, 1998.

CLASS ASSIGNMENTS

| Teacher Name | Class and Section | School Year | Semester |

#	Assignment	Description
1		
2		
3		
4		
5		
6		
7		
8		
9		
10		
11		
12		
13		
14		
15		
16		
17		
18		
19		
20		
21		
22		

Thinking Inside the Block: The Teacher's Day-Planner
by P. Robbins and L. Herndon. Copyright © Corwin Press, 1998.

CLASS ASSIGNMENTS

Teacher Name	Class and Section	School Year	Semester

#	Assignment	Description

Thinking Inside the Block: The Teacher's Day-Planner
by P. Robbins and L. Herndon. Copyright © Corwin Press, 1998.

CLASS ASSIGNMENTS

Teacher Name	Class and Section	School Year	Semester

#	Assignment	Description
1		
2		
3		
4		
5		
6		
7		
8		
9		
10		
11		
12		
13		
14		
15		
16		
17		
18		
19		
20		
21		
22		

Thinking Inside the Block: The Teacher's Day-Planner
by P. Robbins and L. Herndon. Copyright © Corwin Press, 1998.

CLASS ASSIGNMENTS

Teacher Name	Class and Section	School Year	Semester

#	Assignment	Description

Thinking Inside the Block: The Teacher's Day-Planner
by P. Robbins and L. Herndon. Copyright © Corwin Press, 1998.

CLASS ASSIGNMENTS

Teacher Name	Class and Section	School Year	Semester

#	Assignment	Description
1		
2		
3		
4		
5		
6		
7		
8		
9		
10		
11		
12		
13		
14		
15		
16		
17		
18		
19		
20		
21		
22		

Thinking Inside the Block: The Teacher's Day-Planner
by P. Robbins and L. Herndon. Copyright © Corwin Press, 1998.

CLASS ASSIGNMENTS

Teacher Name	Class and Section	School Year	Semester

#	Assignment	Description

Thinking Inside the Block: The Teacher's Day-Planner
by P. Robbins and L. Herndon. Copyright © Corwin Press, 1998.

CLASS GRADES

Teacher Name	Class and Section	School Year	Semester

Month/Date															
Assignments	1	2	3	4	5	6	7	8	9	10	11	12	13	14	15
Student Name															

Thinking Inside the Block: The Teacher's Day-Planner
by P. Robbins and L. Herndon. Copyright © Corwin Press, 1998.

CLASS GRADES

Teacher Name	Class and Section	School Year	Semester

Month/Date
Assignments
Student Name

Thinking Inside the Block: The Teacher's Day-Planner
by P. Robbins and L. Herndon. Copyright © Corwin Press, 1998.

CLASS GRADES

Teacher Name	Class and Section	School Year	Semester

Month/Date													
Assignments													
Student Name													

Thinking Inside the Block: The Teacher's Day-Planner
by P. Robbins and L. Herndon. Copyright © Corwin Press, 1998.

CLASS GRADES

| Teacher Name | Class and Section | School Year | Semester |

| Month/Date |
| Assignments |
| Student Name |

Thinking Inside the Block: The Teacher's Day-Planner
by P. Robbins and L. Herndon. Copyright © Corwin Press, 1998.

CLASS GRADES

Teacher Name	Class and Section	School Year	Semester

Month/Date															
Assignments	1	2	3	4	5	6	7	8	9	10	11	12	13	14	15
Student Name															

Thinking Inside the Block: The Teacher's Day-Planner
by P. Robbins and L. Herndon. Copyright © Corwin Press, 1998.

CLASS GRADES

Teacher Name	Class and Section	School Year	Semester

Month/Date

Assignments

Student Name

Thinking Inside the Block: The Teacher's Day-Planner
by P. Robbins and L. Herndon. Copyright © Corwin Press, 1998.

CLASS GRADES

Teacher Name	Class and Section	School Year	Semester

Month/Date
Assignments
Student Name

Thinking Inside the Block: The Teacher's Day-Planner
by P. Robbins and L. Herndon. Copyright © Corwin Press, 1998.

CLASS GRADES

Teacher Name	Class and Section	School Year	Semester

Month/Date

Assignments

Student Name

Thinking Inside the Block: The Teacher's Day-Planner
by P. Robbins and L. Herndon. Copyright © Corwin Press, 1998.

CLASS GRADES

Teacher Name	Class and Section	School Year	Semester

Month/Date															
Assignments	1	2	3	4	5	6	7	8	9	10	11	12	13	14	15
Student Name															

Thinking Inside the Block: The Teacher's Day-Planner
by P. Robbins and L. Herndon. Copyright © Corwin Press, 1998.

CLASS GRADES

| Teacher Name | Class and Section | School Year | Semester |

Month/Date

Assignments

Student Name

Thinking Inside the Block: The Teacher's Day-Planner
by P. Robbins and L. Herndon. Copyright © Corwin Press, 1998.

CLASS GRADES

Teacher Name	Class and Section	School Year	Semester

Month/Date
Assignments
Student Name

Thinking Inside the Block: The Teacher's Day-Planner
by P. Robbins and L. Herndon. Copyright © Corwin Press, 1998.

CLASS GRADES

| Teacher Name | Class and Section | School Year | Semester |

Month/Date
Assignments
Student Name

Thinking Inside the Block: The Teacher's Day-Planner
by P. Robbins and L. Herndon. Copyright © Corwin Press, 1998.

LESSON PLANNING FORMS

Suggestions for Use

The following planning forms are designed to assist with alignment of the lesson being taught, assessment and standards, and benchmarks. For those teachers using the block schedule, these forms will help them organize the curriculum to account for loss of time in changing from a traditional schedule to a block schedule. Some teachers have begun by distinguishing between essential learning and the "nice to know," in order to focus on key curricular concepts and accommodate the block schedule.

These forms can be very helpful when teaching a course the second time around. Many teachers can teach a course more than once in the same school year during a block schedule. Changes and revisions can be made on the forms as the year progresses, and these planning pages can later become the foundation for curriculum revision and rewrites.

The course planner allows one to organize the entire course content into units that are further broken into topics. A list of materials can be assembled for the course. The standards and benchmarks for students to achieve can be recorded in the last column. With this in place, some teachers then develop a

LESSON PLANNING FORMS

monthly plan from which to work.

The monthly planner has space to list the chapters to be addressed and a memo column to add things such as videos to be shown, purchases to be made, items to be assembled, copies of handouts to be made, and so forth. The monthly plan can also assist teachers with time management issues by planning ahead.

Using the information gathered from the course and monthly planners, some teachers have then developed their weekly and daily lesson plans. These two forms provide the needed information for alignment of instruction with assessment and standards. The Strategies column serves as a handy reminder to incorporate at least three or four strategies in a block of time. Research has shown that the use of several strategies during an extended period of time is essential to prolonging student attention and maximizing retention.

Six copies of each form have been provided in the following section. Please feel free to make as many copies as needed to complete a school year.

COURSE PLANNING

Course Title: _____ Semester/Block: _____

Unit	Topics	Materials	Standards & Benchmarks

Thinking Inside the Block: The Teacher's Day-Planner by P. Robbins and L. Herndon. Copyright © Corwin Press, 1998.

COURSE PLANNING Course Title: _____ Semester/Block: _____

Unit	Topics	Materials	Standards & Benchmarks

Thinking Inside the Block: The Teacher's Day-Planner by P. Robbins and L. Herndon. Copyright © Corwin Press 1998

COURSE PLANNING Course Title: _____ Semester/Block: _____

Unit	Topics	Materials	Standards & Benchmarks

Thinking Inside the Block: The Teacher's Day-Planner by P. Robbins and L. Herndon. Copyright © Corwin Press, 1998.

COURSE PLANNING Course Title: _____ Semester/Block: _____

Unit	Topics	Materials	Standards & Benchmarks

Thinking Inside the Block: The Teacher's Day-Planner
by P. Robbins and L. Herndon. Copyright © Corwin Press, 1998.

COURSE PLANNING Course Title: **Semester/Block:**

Unit	Topics	Materials	Standards & Benchmarks

Thinking Inside the Block: The Teacher's Day-Planner
by P. Robbins and L. Herndon. Copyright © Corwin Press, 1998.

COURSE PLANNING Course Title: _____ Semester/Block: _____

Unit	Topics	Materials	Standards & Benchmarks

Thinking Inside the Block: The Teacher's Day-Planner by P. Robbins and L. Herndon. Copyright © Corwin Press, 1998.

MONTHLY LESSON PLAN Course Title: Semester/Block:

Month	Units	Topics	Chapters	Memo

Thinking Inside the Block: The Teacher's Day-Planner
by P. Robbins and L. Herndon. Copyright © Corwin Press, 1998.

MONTHLY LESSON PLAN Course Title: _____ Semester/Block: _____

Month	Units	Topics	Chapters	Memo

Thinking Inside the Block: The Teacher's Day-Planner by P. Robbins and I. Herndon. Copyright © Corwin Press, 1998.

MONTHLY LESSON PLAN Course Title: Semester/Block:

Month	Units	Topics	Chapters	Memo

Thinking Inside the Block: The Teacher's Day-Planner
by P. Robbins and L. Herndon. Copyright © Corwin Press, 1998.

MONTHLY LESSON PLAN Course Title: Semester/Block:

Month	Units	Topics	Chapters	Memo

Thinking Inside the Block: The Teacher's Day-Planner by R. Robbins and L. Herndon. Copyright © Corwin Press, 1998.

MONTHLY LESSON PLAN Course Title: _____ Semester/Block: _____

Month	Units	Topics	Chapters	Memo

Thinking Inside the Block: The Teacher's Day-Planner by P. Robbins and L. Herndon. Copyright © Corwin Press, 1998.

MONTHLY LESSON PLAN Course Title: _____ Semester/Block: _____

Month	Units	Topics	Chapters	Memo

Thinking Inside the Block: The Teacher's Day-Planner by P. Robbins and L. Herndon. Copyright © Corwin Press, 1998.

WEEKLY LESSON PLAN Course Title: Semester/Block:

Date	Topic	Strategies	Assessment	Standards/Benchmarks
Mon.				
Tues.				
Wed.				
Thur.				
Fri.				

Thinking Inside the Block: The Teacher's Day-Planner by P. Robbins and L. Herndon. Copyright © Corwin Press, 1998.

WEEKLY LESSON PLAN Course Title: _____   Semester/Block: _____

Date	Topic	Strategies	Assessment	Standards/Benchmarks
Mon.				
Tues.				
Wed.				
Thur.				
Fri.				

Thinking Inside the Block: The Teacher's Day-Planner by P. Robbins and L. Herndon. Copyright © Corwin Press, 1998.

WEEKLY LESSON PLAN Course Title: _____ **Semester/Block:** _____

Date	Topic	Strategies	Assessment	Standards/Benchmarks
Mon.				
Tues.				
Wed.				
Thur.				
Fri.				

Thinking Inside the Block: The Teacher's Day-Planner by P. Robbins and L. Herndon. Copyright © Corwin Press, 1998.

WEEKLY LESSON PLAN Course Title: _____ Semester/Block: _____

Date	Topic	Strategies	Assessment	Standards/Benchmarks
Mon.				
Tues.				
Wed.				
Thur.				
Fri.				

Thinking Inside the Block: The Teacher's Day-Planner by P. Robbins and L. Herndon. Copyright © Corwin Press, 1998.

WEEKLY LESSON PLAN Course Title: _____ Semester/Block: _____

Date	Topic	Strategies	Assessment	Standards/Benchmarks
Mon.				
Tues.				
Wed.				
Thur.				
Fri.				

Thinking Inside the Block: The Teacher's Day-Planner by P. Robbins and L. Herndon. Copyright © Corwin Press, 1998.

WEEKLY LESSON PLAN

Course Title: _____ **Semester/Block:** _____

Date	Topic	Strategies	Assessment	Standards/Benchmarks
Mon.				
Tues.				
Wed.				
Thur.				
Fri.				

Thinking Inside the Block: The Teacher's Day-Planner by P. Robbins and L. Herndon. Copyright © Corwin Press, 1998.

DAILY LESSON PLAN

Course Title: **Semester/Block:**

Time Allotted	Topic	Strategies	Assessment	Standards/Benchmarks

Thinking Inside the Block: The Teacher's Day-Planner by P. Robbins and L. Herndon. Copyright © Corwin Press, 1998.

DAILY LESSON PLAN Course Title: Semester/Block:

Time Allotted	Topic	Strategies	Assessment	Standards/Benchmarks

Thinking Inside the Block: The Teacher's Day-Planner by P. Robbins and L. Herndon. Copyright © Corwin Press, 1998.

DAILY LESSON PLAN

Course Title: **Semester/Block:**

Time Allotted	Topic	Strategies	Assessment	Standards/Benchmarks

Thinking Inside the Block: The Teacher's Day-Planner by P. Robbins and L. Herndon. Copyright © Corwin Press, 1998.

DAILY LESSON PLAN Course Title: Semester/Block:

Time Allotted	Topic	Strategies	Assessment	Standards/Benchmarks

Thinking Inside the Block: The Teacher's Day-Planner

DAILY LESSON PLAN Course Title: Semester/Block:

Time Allotted	Topic	Strategies	Assessment	Standards/Benchmarks

Thinking Inside the Block: The Teacher's Day-Planner by P. Robbins and L. Herndon. Copyright © Corwin Press, 1998.

DAILY LESSON PLAN Course Title: _____ Semester/Block: _____

Time Allotted	Topic	Strategies	Assessment	Standards/Benchmarks

Thinking Inside the Block: The Teacher's Day-Planner by P. Robbins and L. Herndon. Copyright © Corwin Press, 1998.

INVENTORY OF TEACHING STRATEGIES

Suggestions for Use

The following inventory provides a space to record teaching strategies, approaches, techniques, contexts, and purposes (review, introduction of a topic, as an energizer, etc.). Building and employing a repertoire of strategies adds interest, vitality, and sometimes movement into lessons. It might also be useful to consider which strategies are best suited to visual, auditory, or tactile/kinesthetic learners. How many of the multiple intelligences are reflected by the strategies listed? Having the strategies listed in one place provides an easily accessible reference for planning.

STRATEGY INVENTORY:

CAN BE USED FOR:

Strategy	Introducing Topic	Processing/Working With New Knowledge	Reviewing Content	Revisiting Previously Taught Concepts

Thinking Inside the Block: The Teacher's Day-Planner by P. Robbins and L. Herndon. Copyright © Corwin Press, 1998.

STRATEGY INVENTORY:

CAN BE USED FOR:

Strategy	Introducing Topic	Processing/Working With New Knowledge	Reviewing Content	Revisiting Previously Taught Concepts

Thinking Inside the Block: The Teacher's Day-Planner by P. Robbins and L. Herndon. Copyright © Corwin Press, 1998.

STRATEGY INVENTORY: CAN BE USED FOR:

Strategy	Introducing Topic	Processing/Working With New Knowledge	Reviewing Content	Revisiting Previously Taught Concepts

Thinking Inside the Block: The Teacher's Day-Planner by P. Robbins and L. Herndon. Copyright © Corwin Press, 1998.

STRATEGY INVENTORY:

CAN BE USED FOR:

Strategy	Introducing Topic	Processing/Working With New Knowledge	Reviewing Content	Revisiting Previously Taught Concepts

Thinking Inside the Block: The Teacher's Day-Planner by P. Robbins and L. Herndon. Copyright © Corwin Press, 1998.

STRATEGY INVENTORY: CAN BE USED FOR:

Strategy	Introducing Topic	Processing/Working With New Knowledge	Reviewing Content	Revisiting Previously Taught Concepts

Thinking Inside the Block: The Teacher's Day-Planner by P. Robbins and L. Herndon. Copyright © Corwin Press, 1998.

STRATEGY INVENTORY: CAN BE USED FOR:

Strategy	Introducing Topic	Processing/Working With New Knowledge	Reviewing Content	Revisiting Previously Taught Concepts

Thinking Inside the Block: The Teacher's Day-Planner by P. Robbins and L. Herndon. Copyright © Corwin Press, 1998.

REFLECTION PAGES

Suggestions for Use

Breaks, during which teachers have an opportunity to reflect upon practices and their outcomes, have been shown to produce new insights and valuable changes, additions, and deletions.

Not all teachers prefer to reflect in the same way. For this reason, the pages that follow offer several options for reflecting on practice.

REFLECTION PAGE

What Worked Well	New Ideas

Additions	Deletions

Thinking Inside the Block: The Teacher's Day-Planner
by P. Robbins and L. Herndon. Copyright © Corwin Press, 1998.

REFLECTION PAGE

What Worked Well	New Ideas

Additions	Deletions

Thinking Inside the Block: The Teacher's Day-Planner
by P. Robbins and L. Herndon. Copyright © Corwin Press, 1998.

REFLECTION PAGE

What Worked Well	New Ideas

Additions	Deletions

Thinking Inside the Block: The Teacher's Day-Planner
by P. Robbins and L. Herndon. Copyright © Corwin Press, 1998.

REFLECTION PAGE

What Worked Well	New Ideas

Additions	Deletions

Thinking Inside the Block: The Teacher's Day-Planner
by P. Robbins and L. Herndon. Copyright © Corwin Press, 1998.

TEACHER NOTES

Thinking Inside the Block: The Teacher's Day-Planner by P. Robbins and L. Herndon. Copyright © Corwin Press, 1998.

TEACHER NOTES

Thinking Inside the Block: The Teacher's Day-Planner by P. Robbins and L. Herndon. Copyright © Corwin Press, 1998.

TIPS: TAKING CARE OF YOURSELF

Teaching is demanding work. Although it provides several pleasures, it also can be exhausting and demanding. The following tips offer suggestions from a whole host of teacher colleagues about how to reenergize and take care of yourself.

- **Allocate at least 10 minutes of quiet time a day for YOU!** Use this time to do what you enjoy. Some people like to sit and reflect. Others like to write in a journal or draw. (Others may find it an ideal time to read a few pages of a great novel, book of poetry, or collection of quotes.)

- **Keep something that is meaningful to you or that makes you happy in or on your desk.** Research shows that when the heart feels stress, the brain waves pick up the sensation of anxiety. It often becomes more difficult to process thoughts when this occurs. Being able to reflect upon something meaningful to you often interrupts unproductive stressful thoughts and feelings and helps put things in perspective.

- **Keep favorite CDs or tapes in your desk** to play while preparing for or reflecting upon the day. Music can serve to energize and invigorate.

- **Schedule time to meet and share with professional colleagues**. Although teachers interact with hundreds of individuals on a weekly basis, unless they are team teaching or work as part of a team, they tend to work in isolation from other adults. Therefore, taking time to meet with colleagues can provide a valuable connection with other adults and an avenue for resources that allows one to work "smarter, not harder."

- **Take time to exercise.** When one is rushing to prepare for class or exhausted after a full day of teaching, it often is difficult to even think about exercise. Yet, exercise can help maintain or even improve one's physical health, as well as clear the mind. Scheduling exercise into your personal calendar -- even for 20 minutes three times a week -- can be a vital investment in you!

- **Keep healthy snacks around.** It is so easy to gorge oneself if a candy jar is handy -- especially if there are treats like these around for students in your classroom! Often when one is tired or rushed, it's easy to grab whatever is easily accessible. Try planning ahead, and bring fresh fruits or vegetables to school. Put them in the refrigerator where they can be available for a cool, crisp, refreshing snack. If this doesn't work for you, try bringing in low-fat, low-sugar treats such as granola bars, pretzels, or some of the cereal mixes now available. Eating well will enable you to enhance your mood through food!

- **Schedule time with friends and family.** Keeping a balance between one's personal and professional life is a powerful way to maintain one's perspective. When one is busy with work, often those who are closest to us get left out of schedules. Spending time in this way can engender a sense of happiness and relaxation.

- **Remember to take time to "smell the roses," as well as the scented markers!** Noticing nature can also renew one's focus. Looking at clouds, flowers, raindrops, trees, or the fish in the aquarium can be a refreshing experience.

Thinking Inside the Block: The Teacher's Day-Planner
by P. Robbins and L. Herndon. Copyright © Corwin Press, 1998.

" A hundred years from now it will not matter the sort of house I lived in, what my bank account was, or the kind of car I drove; but the world may be different because I was important in the life of a child."

- Anonymous

To order more copies of this book, fill out the form below!

ORDER FORM
D8825

(For faster service, photocopy this form and send with your P.O.)

CORWIN PRESS, INC.
A Sage Publications Company
2455 Teller Road
Thousand Oaks, CA 91320-2218
Federal ID Number 77-0260369
(Professional books may be tax-deductible.)

Call: 805-499-9774
Fax: 805-499-0871
E-mail: order@corwinpress.com
www.corwinpress.com

Ship to

Name _____

Institution _____

Address _____ No. _____

City _____ State _____ ZIP+4 _____

Country _____ Telephone (_____) _____
(Required for credit card and institutional purchases)

Bill to (if different) _____ P.O.# _____
(Actual Purchase Order must accompany order.)

Institution _____

Attn: _____

Address _____ No. _____

City _____ State _____ ZIP+4 _____

Country _____ Telephone (_____) _____
(Required for credit card and institutional purchases)

Method of Payment

☐ Check # _____   ☐ VISA   ☐ MasterCard   ☐ Discover

Account Number _____ Exp. Date _____

Signature _____

Qty.	Book No.	Title	Unit Price	Amount
	6783-7 (Paper)	Thinking Inside the Block*	$22.95	
	6782-9 (Library Edition)	Thinking Inside the Block*	$51.95	
	6780-2 (Paper)	Thinking Inside the Block: The Teacher's Day-Planner	$24.95	
	6781-0 (Kit)	Thinking Inside the Block Kit,* includes *Thinking Inside the Block* (paper) and *Teacher's Day-Planner*	$39.95	

☐ YES! Please send me Corwin's complete catalog.   **FREE**

Thinking Inside the Block book and Kit available Spring, 1999.

Shipping and handling charges: U.S. orders add $3.50 for the first book and $1.00 for each additional book; Canadian orders add $10.00 for the first book and $2.00 for each additional book. These charges apply to all orders, including purchase orders and those prepaid by check or credit card. All domestic orders are shipped Ground Parcel unless otherwise requested. In Canada, please add 7% GST (12978 6448 RT) and remit in U.S. dollars. Discounts are available for quantity orders — call Customer Service.

Total Book Order _____

In CA and NY, add appl. Sales Tax _____

In IL, add 6¼% Sales Tax _____

In MA, add 5% Sales Tax _____

In Canada, add 7% GST _____

Subtotal _____

Shipping and Handling _____

Total Amount Due _____

In compliance with GPSR, should you have any concerns about the safety of this product, please advise: International Associates Auditing & Certification Limited The Black Church, St Mary's Place, Dublin 7, D07 P4AX Ireland EUAR@ie.ia-net.com

www.ingramcontent.com/pod-product-compliance
Lightning Source LLC
Chambersburg PA
CBHW081356290426
44110CB00018B/2392